Charl

By United Library

https://campsite.bio/unitedlibrary

Table of Contents

Table of Contents 2

Disclaimer 4

Introduction 5

Charlie Chaplin 8

Biography... 11

Film debut (1914-1917) 17

First National (1918-1922) 24

United Artists (1923-1938)... 28

Controversy and waning popularity (1939-1952).................. 36

European years (1953-1977) 45

Analysis of his work.. 52

Filmography 60

Recognition 63

Other books by United Library 70

Disclaimer

This biography book is a work of nonfiction based on the public life of a famous person. The author has used publicly available information to create this work. While the author has thoroughly researched the subject and attempted to depict it accurately, it is not meant to be an exhaustive study of the subject. The views expressed in this book are those of the author alone and do not necessarily reflect those of any organization associated with the subject. This book should not be taken as an endorsement, legal advice, or any other form of professional advice. This book was written for entertainment purposes only.

Introduction

Charlie Chaplin's readers are invited to step into the extraordinary life and career of Sir Charles Spencer Chaplin, the legendary English comic actor, filmmaker, and composer who left an indelible mark on the world of entertainment. This meticulously researched biography paints a vivid portrait of a man who rose from a childhood of poverty and hardship in Victorian London to become one of the most iconic figures in film history.

Chaplin's journey from the workhouses of his youth to the bright lights of music halls and later, the silver screen, is a testament to his resilience and talent. With the creation of his iconic Tramp persona, he captured the hearts of audiences worldwide, ushering in the era of silent film. As his career blossomed, he took creative control and founded United Artists, solidifying his status as a pioneer in the film industry.

The book delves into Chaplin's groundbreaking films, from the heartfelt "The Kid" to the timeless classics "The Gold Rush" and "City Lights." It explores his refusal to transition to sound films immediately and his audacious satire of Adolf Hitler in "The Great Dictator."

Chaplin's life was not without controversy, and the book candidly discusses the accusations of communist sympathies, scandalous paternity suits, and marriages to younger women that marked the 1940s. Forced into exile and settling in Switzerland, Chaplin's later films showcased his evolving artistic vision.

This book offers an intimate look at the man behind the iconic Tramp character, highlighting his perfectionism, artistic innovation, and lasting impact on the art of filmmaking. This biography pays tribute to a true cinematic genius whose work continues to be celebrated and cherished by audiences worldwide.

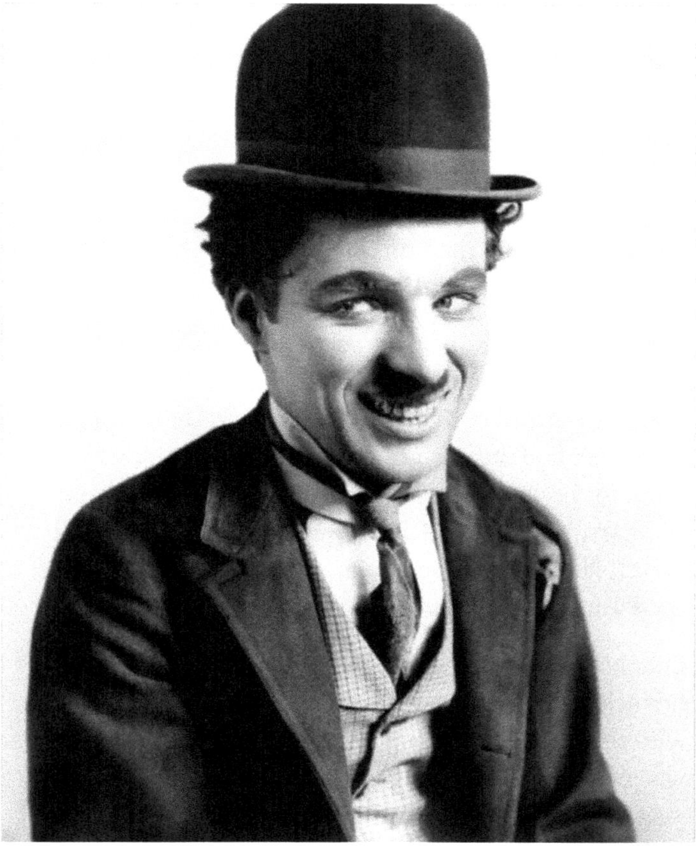

Charlie Chaplin

Charles Spencer Chaplin, known as Charlie Chaplin, was a British actor, director, screenwriter, producer and composer. He was born on April 16, 1889, probably in London (UK), and died on December 25, 1977 in Corsier-sur-Vevey (Switzerland).

From the mid-1910s onwards, he became a silent film idol, particularly in burlesque, thanks to his character The Tramp (referred to simply as "the tramp" in the original versions), and went on to gain wider recognition and fame for his acting and filmmaking. In a career spanning 65 years, he appeared in over 80 films. His public and private life, and the positions he took, were the subject of both adulation and controversy.

Chaplin grew up in poverty with an absent father and a financially troubled mother, both music-hall performers who separated two years after his birth. Later, his mother was committed to a psychiatric hospital when her son was 14. At the age of 5, he made his first stage appearance. He began performing in music halls at an early age and soon became an actor. At 19, he was noticed by impresario Fred Karno and toured the United States. He played his first film role in 1914, in the film *To Make a Living*, and worked with the Essanay, Mutual and

First National production companies. By 1918, he was one of the world's best-known personalities.

In 1919, Chaplin co-founded the United Artists company, gaining total control over his work. His first feature films included *The Tramp* (1918), *The Kid* (1921), *Public Opinion* (1923), *The Gold Rush* (1925) and *The Circus* (1928). He refused to switch to sound cinema and continued to produce silent films in the 1930s, such as *Les Lumières de la ville* (1931) and *Les Temps modernes* (1936). His films then became more political, notably *Le Dictateur* (1940), in which he mocked Hitler and Mussolini. His popularity declined in the 1940s due to controversies surrounding his affairs with women much younger than himself, and a paternity suit. Chaplin was also accused of Communist sympathies, and FBI and Congressional investigations led to the loss of his American visa. He chose to settle in Switzerland in 1952. He abandoned his Tramp character in his last films, including *Monsieur Verdoux* (1947), *Les Feux de la rampe* (1952), *Un roi à New York* (1957) and *La Comtesse de Hong-Kong* (1967).

Chaplin wrote, directed and produced most of his films, as well as acting in them and composing the music. He was a perfectionist, and his financial independence enabled him to devote several years to the development of each of his works. Although his films are *slapstick* comedies, they also contain elements of pathos, social and political themes and autobiographical elements. In 1972, the Academy of Motion Picture Arts and Sciences awarded him an honorary Oscar for his invaluable contribution to the film industry, and several of his feature films are now considered among the greatest in cinema history.

Biography

Youth (1889-1913)

Charles Spencer Chaplin, was born on April 16, 1889, the second child of Hannah Chaplin née Hill (1865-1928) and Charles Chaplin, Sr. (1863-1901). According to David Robinson, Charlie Chaplin's official biographer, his paternal branch was of Huguenot origin: "The Chaplin family lived for generations in Suffolk. The name suggests that they were descended from Huguenots, who had settled in East Anglia in large numbers since the late seventeenth[e] century, ." His birth certificate has not been found in the civil registers, but Chaplin considered that he was born in a house on East Street in the Walworth district of South London, . In 2011, a 1970 letter to Chaplin was rediscovered, claiming that he was born to a gypsy family in Smethwick, Staffordshire, and Chaplin's son Michael suggested that the information was important enough for his father to keep the missive. Regarding his date of birth, Chaplin estimated that he was born on April 16, but an advertisement in the April 11, 1889 edition of *The Magnet* newspaper states the 15th. Four years earlier, his parents had married and Charles Sr. recognized Sydney John, a son from Hannah's previous relationship with an unknown man. At the time of his birth, Chaplin's parents were both music-hall performers.

His mother, the daughter of a shoemaker, had a relatively unsuccessful career under the stage name Lily Harley, while his father, the son of a butcher, was a popular singer. They separated around 1891, and the following year Hannah gave birth to her third son, Wheeler Dryden, from a relationship with music-hall singer Leo Dryden; the child was taken away by his father at the age of six months and remained estranged from Chaplin for thirty years.

Chaplin's childhood was marked by hardship and deprivation, leading his official biographer David Robinson to describe it as "the most spectacular tale ever told of the rise from rags to riches". His early years were spent with his mother and brother Sydney in the London borough of Kennington; apart from some sewing and nannying, Hannah had no income, and Charles Sr. provided no support for his children. As the household's financial situation deteriorated, Chaplin was sent to a *workhouse at the age of* seven. He later described his life there as "a sad existence" and was briefly returned to his mother 18 months later; Hannah was soon forced to separate from her children once again, who were sent to another institution for destitute children.

In September 1898, Chaplin's mother was admitted to Cane Hill Lunatic Asylum after developing a psychosis apparently brought on by malnutrition and syphilis.

During the two months of her hospitalization, Chaplin and his brother were sent to live with their father, whom they hardly knew. Charles Sr. sank into alcoholism, and his behavior led to a visit from a child welfare organization. He died of cirrhosis two years later, at the age of 38.

Hannah's health improved, but she suffered a relapse in May 1903. Chaplin, then aged 14, takes her to the dispensary, from where she is sent back to Cane Hill. He lived alone for several days, sleeping on the streets while waiting for his brother, who had joined the Navy two years earlier, to return" . Hannah left the asylum after eight months, but relapsed permanently in March 1905. Chaplin later wrote: "We could do nothing but accept our poor mother's fate." In 1921, Charlie and his brother Sydney obtained permission to take her with them to Hollywood. Charlie bought her a house by the sea, and Hannah lived out her last seven years there, cared for at home. It was here that she was able to see her third son, Wheeler Dryden, from whom she had been separated for thirty years. She died on August 28, 1928.

First services

Chaplin began performing on stage at an early age. He made his first appearance at the age of five, replacing Hannah in a show in Aldershot. It was an exception, but his mother encouraged him and "imbued him with the feeling [that] he had some kind of talent". Through his father's connections, he became a member of the Eight Lancashire Lads dance troupe, performing in British music halls in 1899 and 1900. Chaplin worked hard and the troupe was popular, but he was not satisfied with dancing and wanted to turn to acting.

When Chaplin was on tour with the Eight Lancashire Lads, his mother made sure he stayed in school, but he dropped out at around thirteen. After a period of odd jobs, at fourteen and shortly after his mother's relapse, he joined an art agency in London's West End. The head of the agency recognized Chaplin's potential and soon offered him his first role as a newspaper salesman in Harry A. Saintsbury's play *Jim, a Romance of Cockayne.* The play premiered in July 1903, but was not a success and performances ended after two weeks; Chaplin's comic performance was nevertheless noticed by critics". Saintsbury then cast him as Billy the bellboy in Charles Frohman's play *Sherlock Holmes.* His performance was so well received that he was called to London to perform alongside William Gillette, who had co-written the play with Arthur Conan Doyle. He made his last tour of *Sherlock Holmes in* early 1906, after playing it for over two and a half years.

Comic actor

Chaplin soon joined another company and starred in a sketch comedy, *Repairs*, with his brother Sydney, who had also embarked on an artistic career. In May 1906, he took part in the children's show *Casey's Circus*, developing his burlesque skills and quickly becoming the star of the play. By the end of the tour in July 1907, the 18-year-old had become an accomplished comedian [ ]. Nevertheless, he had difficulty finding work, and a brief foray into stand-up did not meet with the success he had hoped for [ ].

Meanwhile, in 1906 Sydney Chaplin joined Fred Karno's prestigious comedy troupe, becoming one of its leading actors in 1908 [ ]. In February, he managed to secure a two-week trial period for his younger brother. Karno was initially unconvinced, regarding Chaplin as a "pale, puny, scowling child" who "seems far too shy to do anything well in the theater". However, he was impressed by his first performance at the London Theatre and hired him immediately. After a number of minor roles, Chaplin moved into the lead in 1909, and in April 1910 he starred in the new comedy *Jimmy the Fearless. It was* a great success that drew the attention of the press to the young artist [ ].

Karno chose him to tour North America with part of his troupe. Chaplin led the music-hall shows, impressing critics who described him as "one of the finest pantomime artists ever seen". The tour lasted 21 months, and the troupe returned to Britain in June 1912. Chaplin then had the unsettling feeling of "returning to depressing platitudes", and was delighted when a new tour began in October'.

Film debut (1914-1917)

Keystone

Now in the sixth month of his American tour, Chaplin was invited to join the New York Motion Picture Company; one of the company's executives had seen one of his shows and thought he could replace Fred Mace, the star of the Keystone studio, who wanted to retire. Chaplin considered Keystone's comedies a "crude mixture" but welcomed the prospect of a new career; in September 1913 he signed a one-year contract with a weekly salary of $150 (about $3,880 in 2023 dollars) .

Chaplin arrived at the Los Angeles studios in early December 1913 and met his manager Mack Sennett, who thought the 24-year-old looked too young. He didn't start acting until the end of February 1914, during which time he familiarized himself with filmmaking. He made his debut in the short film *Pour gagner sa vie*, released on February 2, 1914, but hated the film. In it, he presented himself as a kind of dandy in a tight frock coat, top hat and large, drooping moustache. For his second role, Chaplin chose the *Tramp* costume with which he made his name; in his autobiography, he describes the process:

"I wanted everything to be a contradiction: the baggy pants, the tight jacket, the narrow hat and wide shoes... I added a little moustache which I thought would age me without affecting my expression. I had no idea of the character, but as soon as I was dressed, the clothes and make-up made me feel who he was. I began to get to know him, and when I walked onto the set, he was entirely born."

This film was *Mabel's Strange Adventure,* but the character of "Charlie Chaplin" appeared for the first time in *Charlot est content de lui*, shot shortly afterwards but released two days earlier, on February 7, 1914. Chaplin quickly adopted the character and made suggestions for the films in which he appeared, suggestions which were rejected by the directors. During the shooting of his 11^e film, *Mabel at the Wheel*, he confronted director Mabel Normand, and the incident almost led to the termination of his contract. Sennett kept him on, however, after receiving orders for new films with Chaplin. He also allows him to direct his next film after Chaplin promises to pay him $1,500 (about $38,287 in 2023 dollars) if he is unsuccessful.

Un béguin de Charlot, released on May 4, 1914, marked Chaplin's directorial debut and was a great success. Thereafter, he directed virtually all the Keystone shorts in which he starred; Chaplin later reported that this period, when he made about one film a week, was the most exciting of his career. He introduced a slower form of comedy than the typical Keystone farces, and quickly gathered a large following . In November 1914, he starred with Marie Dressler in the feature film *Le Roman comique de Charlot et Lolotte* directed by Sennett; the film was a success and increased his popularity. When Chaplin's contract expired at the end of the year, he asked for a weekly salary of $1,000 (about $25,525 in 2023 dollars), a sum Sennett refused as too high.

Essanay

The Essanay Film Manufacturing Company offered Chaplin a weekly salary of $1,250 (about $31,591 in 2023 dollars) with a $10,000 signing bonus. He joined the studio at the end of December 1914, joining other actors such as Leo White, Bud Jamison, Paddy McGuire and Billy Armstrong. While looking for a supporting actress for his second film, *Charlot fait la noce*, he spotted a secretary named Edna Purviance in a San Francisco café. He hired her and she acted in 35 films with him; they also had a romantic affair that lasted until 1917.

Chaplin exerted considerable control over his films, and began to devote considerable time and energy to each of his productions . A month separated his second production, *Charlot fait la noce*, and his third, *Charlot boxeur,* and he adopted this rhythm for his later productions with Essenay. He also modified his character, criticized by Keystone for being "malicious, boorish and rude", to give him a softer, more romantic personality. This evolution is illustrated by *Le Vagabond* in April 1915, and *Charlot garçon de banque* in August, both of which feature a sadder ending. This was an innovation for comedy films, and serious critics began to appreciate his work more. With Essanay, Chaplin finds the themes that define the world of Charlie Chaplin.

Immediately after his film debut, Chaplin became a cultural phenomenon. Stores sold products associated with his character, Charlie Chaplin, who appeared in comic strips and songs". By July 1915, according to a reporter for *Motion Picture* Magazine, "Chaplinitis" was spreading in America. His popularity also spread abroad, and he became the first international film star. When his contract with Essenay expired in December 1915, Chaplin, fully aware of his celebrity status, asked his new studio for a signing bonus of $150,000 (about $3,790,954 in 2023 dollars). He received several offers from Universal, Fox and Vitagraph, among others.

Mutual

He was finally hired by the Mutual studio, which paid him an annual salary of $670,000 (about $16,932,928 in 2023 dollars), making Chaplin, then aged 26, one of the highest paid people in the world. This high sum shocked the public and was widely reported in the press. Studio president John R. Freuler explains that they can afford to pay Chaplin this salary because "the public wants Chaplin and will pay to see him".

Mutual granted Chaplin his own studio in Los Angeles, which opened in March 1916. He recruited two new actors to accompany him, Albert Austin and Eric Campbell, and made a series of more elaborate, melodramatic films: *Charlot the Department Head*, *Charlot the Fireman*, *Charlot the Musician*, *Charlot Coming Home Late*, *Charlot and the Count*. For *Charlot the loan shark,* he hired actor Henry Bergman, who worked with him for 30 years. *Charlot fait du ciné* and *Charlot patine* were his last productions for 1916. His contract with Mutual stipulated that he was to make a short film every four weeks, a commitment he kept. However, he began to ask for more time to create his films, and made only four more for Mutual in the first ten months of 1917: *Charlot policeman*, *Charlot fait une cure*, *L'Émigrant* and *Charlot s'évade*. Because of their meticulous direction and careful construction, these films are considered some of Chaplin's best work by film specialists[m]. For Chaplin, his years at Mutual were the happiest of his career.

Chaplin is criticized by the British press for not taking part in the First World War. He replies that he volunteers to fight for the UK if called up, and that he has already answered the American conscription; neither country asks him to enlist, and the British Embassy in the US issues a statement saying that Chaplin "is far more useful to Britain earning money and buying war bonds than in the trenches". Despite this criticism, Chaplin is one of the soldiers' favorite actors, and his popularity continues to grow worldwide. The American magazine *Harper's Weekly* reports that Charlie Chaplin's name is "part of the lingua franca of almost every country" and that the image of Chaplin is "universally familiar". By 1917, Chaplin's professional impersonators were so widespread that he took legal action, and it was reported that nine out of ten men attending costume parties took up his get-up. Actress Minnie M. Fiske writes that "an ever-increasing number of educated people are beginning to regard the young English buffoon, Charlie Chaplin, as an extraordinary artist and comic genius".

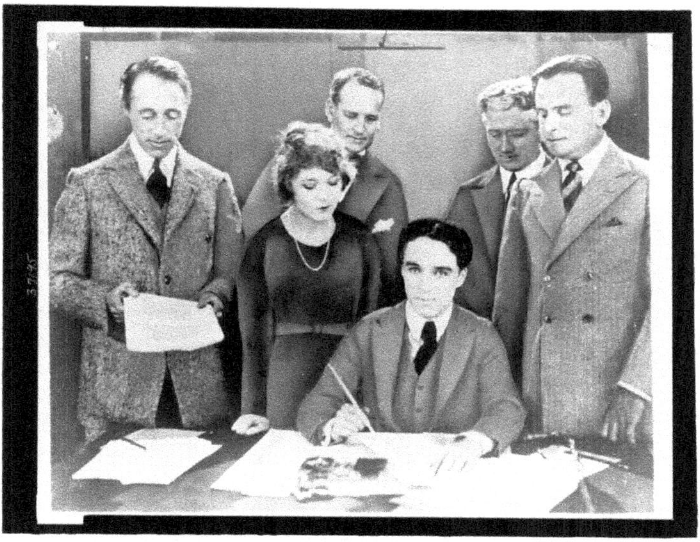

First National (1918-1922)

Mutual did not take kindly to Chaplin's reduced output, and the contract ended amicably. For his new studio, his main objective was to have greater independence; his brother Sydney, now his artistic agent, told the press that "Chaplin must be allowed to have all the time and money he needs to produce films in his own way... It's quality, not quantity, that we want". In June 1917, Chaplin signed a million-dollar contract (about $19,955,844 in 2023 dollars) for eight films with the theater owners' association First National Pictures. He decides to build his own studio on a 5-acre plot (20,200 m^2) near Sunset Boulevard with the best facilities and equipment available. The studio opened in January 1918, and Chaplin was given a great deal of freedom to make his films.

A Dog's Life, released in April 1918, is his first film under this new contract. It shows his growing attention to plot and his treatment of Charlie the Tramp as a kind of Pierrot. The film was described by French critic Louis Delluc as "cinema's first total work of art". Chaplin then took part in the war effort, touring the U.S. for a month to raise funds for the Allies. He also produced a short propaganda film for the government called *The Bond*. His next film, *Charlot soldat*, featured Charlot in the trenches; his associates warned him against making a comedy about war, but he thought otherwise: "dangerous or not, the idea excited me". Shooting lasted four months, and the 45-minute film was a great success when it was released in October 1918.

After the release of *The Tramp,* Chaplin asked First National for more funds, but was refused. Frustrated by the studio's lack of regard for quality, and worried by rumors of a merger with Famous Players-Lasky , he approached his colleagues Douglas Fairbanks, Mary Pickford and D. W. Griffith to found a new distribution company. The creation of United Artists in January 1919 was a revolution for the film industry, as the four founders could now personally finance their works and have total control over them. Chaplin was eager to get started with his new company and offered to buy out his contract with First National. The studio refused, insisting that he deliver the last six films he had promised.

Before United Artists was founded, Chaplin married for the first time. The 17-year-old actress Mildred Harris was pregnant, and they married discreetly in Los Angeles in September 1918 to avoid controversy; the pregnancy turned out to be false. Chaplin was unhappy with the union, which he felt affected his creativity, and the production of *An Idyll in the Fields* proved difficult . Harris then became pregnant for real, and gave birth to a son on July 7, 1919. The newborn, Norman Spencer Chaplin, was malformed and died three days later. The couple divorced in April 1920, and Chaplin explains in his autobiography that they were "absolutely not made for each other" .

This personal tragedy influenced Chaplin's work, as he planned to make Charlie the guardian of a young boy . Shooting of The *Kid* began in August 1919 with four-year-old Jackie Coogan. Chaplin realized that the project was bigger than expected and, to appease First National, halted production and quickly shot *A Day of Pleasure*. The making of The *Kid lasted* nine months, until May 1920, and its 68-minute running time made it the filmmaker's longest to date. Marked by themes of poverty and separation, *The Kid is* considered to be influenced by Chaplin's own childhood, and is one of the first films to combine comedy and drama. The film was an immediate success on its release in January 1921, and was distributed in over 50 countries over the following three years.

Chaplin devoted five months to his next 31-minute film, *Charlie Chaplin and the Iron Mask*. After its release in September 1921, he decided to return to Britain for the first time in almost a decade. He then fulfilled his contract with First National, making *Payday* in February 1922 and *The Pilgrim* a year later.

United Artists (1923-1938)

Public Opinion* and *the Gold Rush

Having fulfilled his obligations to First National, Chaplin was now free to make his films as an independent producer. In November 1922, he began shooting *Public Opinion*. He wanted this romantic drama to launch Edna Purviance's career, and made only a brief uncredited cameo in the production. Wanting the film to be realistic, he asked his actors to act in a restrained manner, explaining that in real life "men and women try to conceal their emotions rather than trying to show them". *L'Opinion publique* premiered in September 1923 to critical acclaim for its subtle, innovative approach. Audiences, however, showed little interest in a Chaplin film without Charlie Chaplin, and the film flopped. Proud of his film, Chaplin was affected by this setback because he had set out to make a dramatic film, and withdrew L'*Opinion publique* from theaters as quickly as possible.

Chaplin returned to acting for his next project, thinking: "This next film must be an epic! the biggest! Inspired by a photograph of the 1898 Klondike Gold Rush and the story of the Donner Expedition of 1846-1847, he made what journalist Geoffrey Macnab called "an epic comedy on a serious subject"[ ]. In *The Gold Rush,* Chaplin is portrayed as a lonely prospector facing adversity and searching for love. With Georgia Hale as his partner, Chaplin began shooting in the mountains of western Nevada in February 1924. The production was complex, with over 600 extras, extravagant sets and special effects; the last scene was not completed until May 1925, after 15 months of shooting.

Costing almost a million dollars, Chaplin considered *The Gold Rush to be* his best film to date. After its release in August 1925, it became one of the biggest successes of silent cinema, grossing five million dollars (around $72,893,738 in 2023)[ ]. The comedy includes some of Chaplin's most famous scenes, such as the one of Charlie eating his shoe or the so-called "bun dance"[ ], and he later declared that he would like people to remember him through this film.

Lita Grey and *Le Cirque*

While directing *The Gold Rush*, Chaplin married for the second time. As with his first marriage, Lita Grey was a young actress who was to appear in the film, and whose unexpected pregnancy forced Chaplin to marry her. At the time, she was 16 and he 35, and under California law this relationship could be classified as statutory rape. According to the divorce papers, Chaplin wanted to have an abortion, but she refused. Lita Grey's mother threatened to report Chaplin to the police if he didn't marry her daughter. So he organized a discreet ceremony in Mexico on November 24, 1924. Lita gave birth to a first son, Charles Chaplin Jr. on May 5, 1925, and a second, Sydney Earle Chaplin, on March 30, 1926.

The union was unhappy, and Chaplin spent a lot of time in the studio to avoid seeing his wife. In November 1926, Lita Grey left their home with their children. During the difficult divorce proceedings, Lita Grey's documents accusing Chaplin of infidelity, violence and "perverse sexual desires" are published in the press" . Chaplin is reported to be on the verge of a nervous breakdown, as the story hits the headlines and groups are formed to call for his films to be banned' . Eager to put an end to the affair, Chaplin's lawyers agreed in August 1927 to pay $600,000 (about $8,831,034 in 2023 dollars), the largest sum awarded in a U.S. trial up to that time. Chaplin's popularity enabled him to overcome the incident, which was quickly forgotten, but he remained deeply affected' .

Before the divorce proceedings began, Chaplin began work on a new film, *Le Cirque*. Shooting was suspended for ten months during the scandal of his divorce, and production was plagued by difficulties. Finally completed in October, *Le Cirque* was released in January 1928 to positive reviews. At the 1re Academy Awards, Chaplin received an honorary Oscar "for his versatility and genius in acting, writing, directing and producing *The Circus*". Despite the film's success, Chaplin associated it with the stress of production; he did not mention it in his autobiography, and found it difficult to work on when he re-released it in 1967.

City Lights

Sound cinema appeared around the same time as *Le Cirque*. Chaplin was skeptical about the new technique, and felt that "talkies" were no match for silent films, from an artistic point of view. He was also reluctant to change the formula that had made him a success and feared that giving Charlie Chaplin a voice would limit his international appeal. He therefore rejected this Hollywood fad and began work on a new silent film; this decision nevertheless made him anxious, and he remained so throughout the production of this new project.

When filming began in late 1928, Chaplin had been working on the story for almost a year. *City Lights* depicts Charlie's love for a blind florist, played by Virginia Cherrill, and his efforts to raise funds for an operation to restore her sight. Chaplin worked "to the verge of madness to achieve perfection", and filming lasted 21 months, until September 1930.

Chaplin completed *City Lights* in December 1930, at a time when silent films had become anachronistic. A pre-screening was unsuccessful, but the press was captivated. One journalist wrote: "No one but Charlie Chaplin could have done it. He is the only one who has that strange something called 'audience appeal' in sufficient quantity to defy the popular penchant for talking pictures". On its official release in January 1931, *City Lights* was a popular and financial success, grossing over three million dollars" . The British Film Institute cited it as Chaplin's greatest achievement, and critic James Agee referred to its finale as "the finest acting and the greatest moment in the history of the cinema" .

Paulette Goddard and *Les Temps modernes*

City Lights was a success, but Chaplin wasn't sure he could make another film without dialogue. He remained convinced that sound would not work in his films, but was also "obsessed by the depressing fear of being old-fashioned". Because of these uncertainties, in early 1931 the actor chose to take a vacation, and stopped shooting for 16 months . He visited Western Europe, including France and Switzerland, and spontaneously decided to travel to the empire of Japan. There, he witnessed the incident of May 15, 1932, during which nationalist officers attempted a coup d'état, assassinating Japanese Prime Minister Tsuyoshi Inukai. The initial plan included killing

Charlie Chaplin in order to start a war with the United States. When the Prime Minister is killed, his son Takeru Inukai attends a sumo competition with Charlie Chaplin, probably saving their lives.

In his autobiography, he notes that on his return to Los Angeles in June 1932, he felt "lost and aimless, tired and conscious of extreme loneliness". He briefly considers the possibility of retiring and moving to China.

Chaplin's loneliness was alleviated when, in July, he met 21-year-old actress Paulette Goddard, with whom he formed a happy couple. Still hesitating whether to make a film, he wrote a serial novel about his travels, which was published in *Woman's Home Companion* magazine. His stay abroad, during which he met several influential figures, had a very stimulating effect on Chaplin, and he became increasingly interested in international issues. The state of American labor during the Great Depression troubled him, and he feared that capitalism and machines would lead to high unemployment. It was these concerns that motivated him to develop his new film.

Modern Times was presented by Chaplin as "a satire of certain situations in our industrial life". He considered making it a talkie, but changed his mind during rehearsals. Like its predecessors, *Modern Times* uses synchronized sound effects, but almost no speech. In the film, Chaplin's "gibberish" rendition of a song nevertheless gives Charlie a voice for the first time. After recording the music, the result was presented in February 1936. It was his first film since *The Kid* to incorporate political and social references, and this aspect generated a great deal of media coverage, even if Chaplin tried to downplay the subject. The film was less successful than his previous films, and critics were more mixed, some disapproving of its political significance . Nevertheless, *Modern Times* has become a classic in Chaplin's repertoire .

Following this outing, Chaplin traveled to the Far East with Goddard. The couple refused to comment on the nature of their relationship, and it was unclear whether they were married or not. Some time later, Chaplin reveals that they were married in Canton, China, during this trip. However, the two soon drifted apart to devote themselves to their work; Goddard finally filed for divorce in 1942, claiming that they had been separated for over a year.

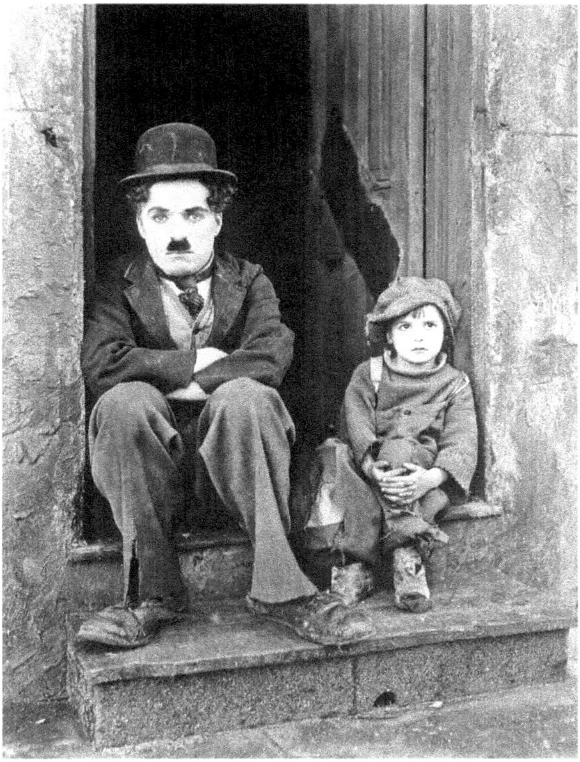

Controversy and waning popularity (1939-1952)

The Dictator

Chaplin was deeply disturbed by the political tensions and rising nationalism in Europe in the 1930s, and felt he could not ignore them in his films. Observers drew parallels with Adolf Hitler: they were born four days apart, both had achieved worldwide fame despite their humble origins, and the German dictator wore the same moustache as Chaplin. This physical resemblance became the basis for Chaplin's next film, *The Great Dictator*, which directly mocked Hitler and fascism""" .

Chaplin spent two years writing the script and began shooting in September 1939, just as the Second World War was breaking out. Chaplin decided to give up silent film, believing it to be outmoded and because it was easier to deliver a political message with the spoken word. Making a comedy about Hitler was a tricky business, but Chaplin's financial independence enabled him to take the risk: "I was determined to do it, because Hitler must be laughed at, ". In the film, Chaplin moves away from his character of Charlie Chaplin, while retaining his get-up, by playing a "Jewish barber" living in a European dictatorship that bears a striking resemblance to Hitler's dictatorship; Chaplin thus responds to Nazi claims that he is Jewish' . Charlie Chaplin also played the dictator "Adenoïd Hynkel", parodying Hitler.

The Great Dictator spent a year in post-production and was released to the public in October 1940. The film is the subject of a major publicity campaign, and a *New York Times* critic calls it the most eagerly awaited film of the year. It enjoyed considerable popular success, even if the ending was controversial' . In this finale, in which his Jewish barber character takes the place of the dictator, Chaplin delivers a six-minute speech to the camera, in which he sets out his personal political views' . According to film historian Charles J. Maland, at a time when cinema was avoiding controversial political themes, this liberty marked the beginning of Chaplin's decline in popularity: "From now on, no fan will be able to separate the political dimension from the film star". *The Great Dictator* was nominated in five categories at the 13^e Academy Awards, including Best Picture, Best Actor and Best Screenplay, although it failed to win a single statuette.

Joan Barry and Oona O'Neill

In the mid-1940s, Chaplin was involved in a series of trials that consumed much of his time and affected his public image. These were linked to his intermittent relationship with aspiring actress Joan Barry, between June 1941 and the summer of 1942. They split up after Barry showed signs of mental illness, and she was arrested twice for harassment after the break-up. She reappeared the following year, announcing that she was pregnant with the director's child; he denied it, and Barry initiated paternity proceedings.

J. Edgar Hoover, director of the Federal Bureau of Investigation (FBI), suspicious of Chaplin's political leanings, exploited the opportunity to damage his reputation. As part of a smear campaign, the FBI indicted him in four related cases. In particular, Chaplin is accused of violating the *Mann Act*, which prohibits the interstate transportation of women for sexual purposes. Historian Otto Friedrich argued that these were "absurd prosecutions" under an "old text", but Chaplin faced up to 23 years in prison. The evidence on three counts proved insufficient to go to trial, but the investigation of the *Mann* Act violation began in March 1944. Chaplin was acquitted two weeks later. The case makes frequent headlines, with *Newsweek* calling it "the biggest public relations scandal since the Roscoe Arbuckle murder trial in 1921".

Barry gave birth to a daughter, Carole Ann, in October 1944, and the paternity trial began in February 1945. After two difficult trials, during which Chaplin was accused of "moral turpitude" by the prosecutor, he was declared the father. The judge refused to accept the medical evidence, in particular the difference in blood type, which invalidated this conclusion, and Chaplin was ordered to pay his daughter alimony until she turned 21. Media coverage of the trial is influenced by the FBI, which passes on information to the influential tabloid journalist Hedda Hopper[*].

The controversy surrounding Chaplin increased further when, on June 16, 1943, two weeks after the paternity proceedings had begun, a new marriage was announced with his new 18-year-old protégée, Oona O'Neill, daughter of American playwright Eugene O'Neill. Chaplin, then 54, had been introduced to her by an art agent seven months earlier, and in his autobiography, he describes their meeting as "the happiest event of [his] life" and says he had discovered "perfect love". They remained married until his death in 1977, and had eight children: Geraldine Leigh (1944), Michael John (1946), Josephine Hannah (1949), Victoria (1951), Eugene Anthony (1953), Jane Cecil (1957), Annette Emily (1959) and Christopher James (1962).

Monsieur Verdoux and accusations of communism

Chaplin argues that these trials have demolished his creativity, and in April 1946 he begins shooting a film he's been working on since 1942. *Monsieur Verdoux* is a black comedy about a French bank clerk, M. Verdoux, played by

Chaplin, who becomes unemployed and starts marrying and murdering rich widows to support his family. The idea came from Orson Welles, who wanted Chaplin to star in a film about French serial killer Henri Désiré Landru. Chaplin thought the concept "would make a superb comedy" and bought the script from Welles for $5,000 (about $65,555 in 2023 dollars).

Chaplin once again expresses his political ideas in *Monsieur Verdoux*, criticizing capitalism, and the film was highly controversial when it was released in April 1947. It was booed at the premiere, and some called for it to be banned. It was the first film in which his character had nothing to do with Charlie Chaplin; it was also the first to be a critical and commercial failure in the United States, and was better received abroad. It was nominated for Best Screenplay at the 20^e Academy Awards. Chaplin was nevertheless proud of his work, writing in his autobiography: "*Monsieur Verdoux* is the most intelligent and brilliant film I have ever made.

Monsieur Verdoux's negative reception was largely the result of Chaplin's changing public image. In addition to the scandal of the Joan Barry affair, he was publicly accused of being a Communist. His political actions intensified during the Second World War, and he campaigned for the opening of a second front to relieve the Soviets. He became close to well-known Communist sympathizers such as Hanns Eisler and Bertolt Brecht, and attended receptions organized by Soviet diplomats in Los Angeles. In the political context of "red scare" prevailing in the United States at the time, such activities meant that Chaplin was, according to Larcher, considered "dangerously progressive and amoral". The FBI, determined to get him out of the country, launched an official investigation against him in 1947.

Chaplin denies being a Communist, and presents himself as a pacifist who believes that the US government's actions to suppress an ideology are an unacceptable violation of civil liberties. Refusing to remain silent on this issue, he openly protests against the trials of American Communist Party members before the *House Un-American Activities Committee* (HUAC) and is summoned by the latter. As his actions were widely reported in the press and the Cold War intensified, his failure to acquire American citizenship was criticized, and some called for his deportation. Mississippi Representative John E. Rankin (en) declared before Congress in June 1947: "His life in Hollywood is harmful to the moral fabric of the United States. [If he is expelled], his repugnant films can be kept out of the eyes of American youth. We must expel him and get rid of him once and for all."

The limelight and expulsion from the United States

Although Chaplin remained politically active in the years following the failure of *Monsieur Verdoux*, his next film about a forgotten vaudeville comedian and a young ballerina in Edwardian London is devoid of political significance. *Les Feux de la rampe* is largely autobiographical, referring to Chaplin's childhood, his parents' life and his loss of popularity in the United States". The cast includes several members of his family, including his eldest children and his half-brother, Wheeler Dryden.

After three years of preparation, filming began in November 1951. He adopted a much more serious tone than in his previous films, and regularly spoke of "melancholy" when explaining the script to his partner Claire Bloom. The film is also notable for the presence of Buster Keaton - his only collaboration with Chaplin.

Chaplin decides to organize the world premiere of Les *Feux de la rampe* in London, where the film is set. Leaving Los Angeles, he indicates that he expects never to be able to return, driven out by McCarthyist America. In New York, he and his family boarded the transatlantic liner HMS *Queen Elizabeth* on September 18, 1952. The next day, U.S. Attorney General James McGranery revoked Chaplin's visa, declaring that he must submit to an interview on his political opinions and moral character before he could return to the United States. Although

McGranery tells the press that he has "a pretty strong case against Chaplin", Maland concludes, based on FBI documents made public in the 1980s, that the US government doesn't really have sufficient evidence to prevent Chaplin's return; it's even likely that he would have been granted a visa had he applied for one. However, when he received a cable informing him of this decision, Chaplin decided to sever all ties with the United States:

"Whether or not I came back to this sad country was of little importance to me. I wanted to tell them that the sooner I was rid of this hateful atmosphere, the better off I'd be, that I was tired of America's insults and moral arrogance."

With all his assets in the U.S., Chaplin made no negative comments in the press, but the affair caused a sensation. While Chaplin and his film were well received in Europe, *Les Feux de la rampe* was largely boycotted in the United States, despite positive reviews. Maland writes that Chaplin's fall from an all-time high in popularity "is perhaps the most spectacular in the history of celebrity in the United States".

European years (1953-1977)

Switzerland and *A King in New York*

Chaplin made no attempt to return to the U.S. after his entry visa was revoked, and sent his wife to Los Angeles to settle his affairs. The couple decided on Switzerland, and in January 1953 the family moved into the Manoir de Ban, a 15-hectare property overlooking Lake Geneva in the commune of Corsier-sur-Vevey. Chaplin put his Beverly Hills residence and studio up for sale in March and returned his visa in April. The following year, his wife renounced her American nationality and became British. He abandoned his last professional ties with the United States in 1955 when he sold his shares in United Artists, which had been in financial difficulties since the early 1940s".

Chaplin remained a controversial figure throughout the 1950s, particularly after receiving the International Peace Prize awarded by the communist World Peace Council, and because of his meetings with China's Zhou Enlai and the Soviet Nikita Khrushchev'. He began developing his first European film, *Un roi à New York*, in 1954. Playing an exiled king seeking asylum in the U.S., Chaplin used his recent problems to write the screenplay. His son, Michael, is portrayed as a boy whose parents are targeted by the FBI, while Chaplin's character is accused of being a Communist. This political satire parodies the actions of HUAC, as well as the consumerism of American society in the 1950s[m]. In his review, playwright John Osborne called it Chaplin's "most acid... and overtly personal" film.

Chaplin founds a new production company called Attica and shoots at the Shepperton studios on the outskirts of London. The shoot was difficult, as he was used to his Hollywood studio and crews, and no longer had an unlimited production period. This had an impact on the quality of the film , which received mixed reviews on its release in September 1957[n]. Chaplin prevented American journalists from attending the Paris premiere and decided not to release the film in the United States. This severely hampered the film's commercial success, even though it was an instant hit in Europe. *A King in New York* was not shown in the U.S. until 1973.

Recent years and renewed interest

From the mid-1950s onwards, Chaplin concentrated on re-editing and re-releasing his old films, as well as protecting his copyright. The first of these reissues was *La Revue de Charlot* (1959), featuring new versions of *Une vie de chien*, *Charlot soldat* and Le *Pèlerin*.

In the U.S., the political atmosphere began to change, and the public's attention shifted from Chaplin's opinions to his films. In July 1962, the *New York Times* published an editorial stating that "we don't think the Republic would be in danger if yesterday's unforgettable little Charlie Chaplin were allowed to walk the gangplank of a ship or plane in an American port". That same month, Chaplin received an honorary Doctor of Letters degree from Oxford and Durham Universities. In November 1963, the Plaza Theater in New York begins a retrospective of Chaplin's films, including *Monsieur Verdoux* and *Les Feux de la rampe*, for which the reviews are far more positive than ten years earlier. September 1964 saw the publication of his memoirs, *Histoire de ma vie*, on which he had been working since 1957. The 500-page book, which focuses on his early years and private life, was a worldwide success, although critics pointed out the lack of information on his film career.

Shortly after the publication of his memoirs, Chaplin began work on *The Countess of Hong Kong* (1967), a romantic comedy based on a screenplay he had written in the 1930s for Paulette Goddard. Set on an ocean liner, the action stars Marlon Brando as an American ambassador and Sophia Loren as a stowaway. The film differed from Chaplin's previous productions in several respects: it was the first to employ technicolor and widescreen resolution, while Chaplin concentrated on directing, appearing on screen only in the minor role of a sick steward. He also signed a distribution contract with Universal Pictures. *The Countess of Hong Kong received* negative reviews on its release in January 1967, and was a commercial failure". Chaplin was deeply affected by this setback, and the film was to be his last.

Chaplin suffered several minor strokes in the late 1950s, marking the beginning of a slow decline in his health. Despite these difficulties, he soon set about writing the script for his new film project, *The Freak*, about a winged girl discovered in South America, a project intended to launch the career of his daughter, Victoria Chaplin. However, poor health prevented him from completing the project, and in the early 1970s Chaplin concentrated instead on re-releasing his earlier films, including *The Kid* and *The Circus*, for which he reworked the soundtrack. In 1971, he was made Commander of the National Order of the Legion of Honor at the Cannes Film Festival, and the following year received a Golden Lion for his career at the Venice Film Festival.

In 1972, the Academy of Motion Picture Arts and Sciences awarded him an honorary Oscar, which Robinson saw as the first sign that the United States "wanted to make amends". Chaplin hesitated to accept, then decided to visit Los Angeles for the first time in twenty years. The visit was widely covered by the media, and at the award ceremony he received a twelve-minute standing ovation, the longest in the history of the Oscars, . Visibly moved, Chaplin accepted the statuette, paying tribute to "the incalculable effect he has had in making motion pictures the art form of this century".

Although Chaplin still had film projects, his health became very fragile in the mid-1970s. Several strokes affected his speech, and he had to use a wheelchair, . His latest achievements include the creation of a pictorial autobiography, *My Life in Pictures* (1974), and the 1976 revival of *L'Opinion publique.* He also appeared in a documentary about his life, *The Gentleman Tramp* (1975), directed by Richard Patterson. In 1975, Queen Elizabeth II knighted him at, .

Death

By October 1977, Chaplin's health had deteriorated to the point where he required constant attention. He died of a stroke in his sleep on the morning of December 25, 1977, at the age of 88. In accordance with his last wishes, a small Anglican funeral service was held on December 27, and he was laid to rest in the Corsier-sur-Vevey cemetery. Among the tributes from the film world, director René Clair wrote: "He was a monument of the cinema", while actor Bob Hope declared: "We were lucky to live in his time".

On March 1er 1978, Chaplin's coffin was exhumed and stolen by two car mechanics, a Pole, Roman Wardas, and a Bulgarian, Gantcho Ganev. Their aim was to extort a ransom of one hundred thousand Swiss francs from Oona Chaplin, so that they could later open a car garage. They were arrested in a major police operation on May 17, 1978, and the coffin was found buried in a cornfield near the village of Noville. It was reburied in the Corsier-sur-Vevey cemetery, and a reinforced concrete vault was added to prevent any further incidents .

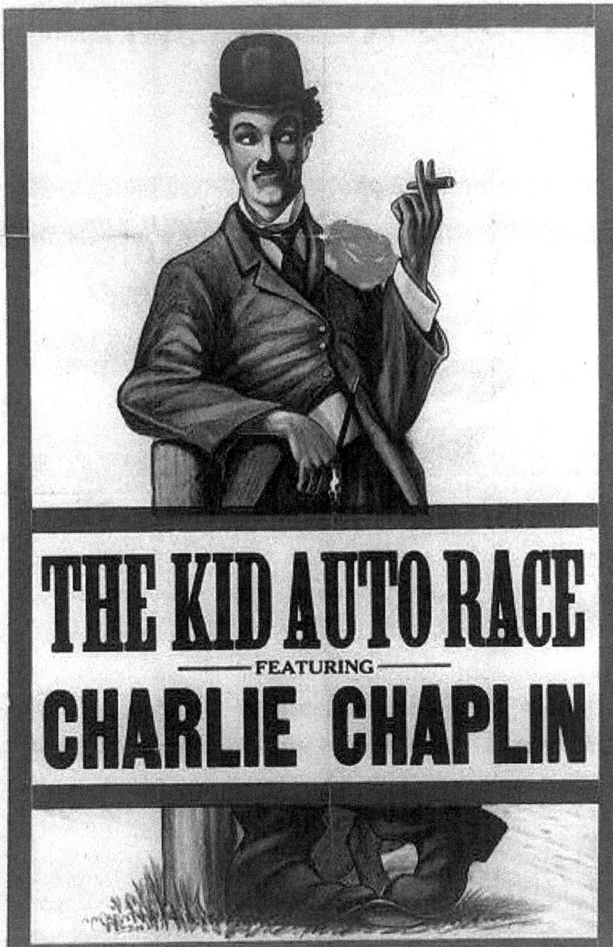
THE KID AUTO RACE
FEATURING
CHARLIE CHAPLIN

Analysis of his work

Influences

Chaplin considered his first inspiration to be his mother, who amused him as a child by sitting at the window and imitating passers-by: "It was from her that I learned not only to express emotions with my hands and face, but also to observe and study people." Chaplin's early years in the music hall enabled him to observe the work of comedians; he also attended Christmas mime shows at the Drury Lane theater, where he studied the art of frivolity with artists such as Dan Leno". His years with Fred Karno's company had a formative effect on his career as an actor and director. He learned to combine tragedy with comedy and to use absurd elements, which became recurrent in his work. In the film industry, Chaplin drew on the work of French comedian Max Linder, whom he admired". In developing Chaplin's costume and acting, he was probably inspired by the American vaudeville scene, where vagabond characters were commonplace.

Methods

Throughout his career, Chaplin said very little about his filmmaking techniques, likening it to revealing his secrets to a magician. Little is known about his working methods, but they have been studied by Kevin Brownlow and David

Gill and skilfully exposed in the documentary series *Unknown Chaplin* (1983).

Before making talkies with *The Great Dictator*, Chaplin never began shooting with a finished script. For his first films, he had only a vague idea, such as "The Tramp goes to a health resort" or "The Tramp works as a pawnbroker". He then had the sets made and worked with the other actors to improvise comic effects, refining the script throughout the production. As ideas are accepted or rejected, a narrative structure emerges, and Chaplin is often forced to flip scenes that run counter to the story. From *L'Opinion publique* onwards, Chaplin began shooting from a pre-established script, but all his films up to *Modern Times* continued to undergo modifications until they reached their final form.

In making films in this way, Chaplin needed more time than any other director of the time. If he runs out of ideas, he takes several days away from the studio, keeping his crews ready as soon as inspiration returns. His perfectionism also slowed down the production process. According to his British friend and director Ivor Montagu, "nothing short of perfection was good enough" for him. Since he personally financed his films, Chaplin had complete freedom to achieve this goal, shooting as many takes as necessary. The number of takes was often excessive: each completed take of *The Kid* required 53 while to shoot the 20 minutes of *The Emigrant*, he used over 12,000 m of film, enough to make a feature-length film.

Describing his production methods as "sheer determination to the brink of madness", Chaplin was usually completely exhausted from shooting. Even in his later years, his work "took precedence over everything and everyone else". The mixture of improvisation and perfectionism that resulted in days of effort and thousands of feet of wasted film proved taxing for Chaplin, leading him to lash out at his actors and crews.

Chaplin exercised complete control over his work, to the point of mimicking other roles so that his actors imitated him exactly. He personally edited all his films, digging through vast quantities of film stock to create the desired film. Nevertheless, Chaplin received help from other artists, including his friend and director of photography Roland Totheroh, his brother Sydney Chaplin and various assistant directors, such as Harry Crocker, Dan James and Charles Reisner.

Style and themes

While Chaplin's comic style is generally referred to as *slapstick*, it is considered restrained and intelligent, and film historian Philip Kemp describes his work as a blend of "graceful physical comedy and thoughtful situational comedy". Chaplin moved away from traditional *slapstick* by slowing the pace of the action and focusing on the viewer's relationship with the characters. The comic effects in Chaplin's films are centered on Charlie's reaction to the things that happen to him: the humor comes not from Charlie running into a tree, but from him lifting his hat in apology. His biographer Dan Kamin writes that Chaplin's "eccentric mannerisms" and his "serious demeanor at the heart of *slapstick*" are other central aspects of his comic style.

Chaplin's silent films generally follow Charlie's efforts to survive in a hostile world. Although he lives in poverty and is frequently mistreated, he remains kind and optimistic; defying his social position, he strives to be seen as a gentleman. The Tramp opposes authority figures and "gives as good as he gets", which led Robinson and Louvish to see him as a representative of the underprivileged: "A Mr. Everyman becoming a heroic savior". Hansmeyer notes that many of Chaplin's films end with "Charlot destitute and alone [walking] optimistically... towards the setting sun... to continue his journey".

The use of pathos is a well-known aspect of Chaplin's work and Larcher notes his ability to "[provoke] laughter and tears". Chaplin sometimes drew on tragic events for his films, as in *The Gold Rush, which was* inspired by the unfortunate fate of the Donner expedition. Chaplin's early comedies portrayed a variety of themes, from greed (*The Gold Rush*) and abandonment (*The Kid*) to more controversial subjects such as immigration (*The Emigrant*) and drugs (*Charlot the Policeman*).

Social commentary is also important in his early films, as he portrays the underprivileged in a positive light and highlights their hardships. Later, he developed a keen interest in economics and felt compelled to share his opinions in his films. *Les Temps modernes* illustrates the difficult working conditions of industrial workers, *Le Dictateur* parodies Hitler and Mussolini and ends with a speech against nationalism, *Monsieur Verdoux* criticizes war and nationalism, while *Un roi à New York* attacks McCarthyism.

Chaplin incorporated many autobiographical elements into his films, and psychologist Sigmund Freud considered that he "always represented himself as he was in his sad childhood". It's generally accepted that *The Kid* reflects the trauma he suffered in an orphanage, while the main character in *Limelight* refers to his parents' lives, and *A King in New York* refers to his expulsion from the United States. His difficult relationship with his mentally ill mother is often reflected in the female characters in his films, and in Charlot's desire to save them.

When it comes to the structure of his films, film historian Gerald Mast sees them as a series of sketches linked by a common thread, rather than a sequence ordered by a precise script. Visually, they are simple and economical, with scenes acted out theatre-style. In his autobiography, Chaplin writes that "simplicity is preferable... pompous effects slow down the action, are dull and unpleasant... The camera must not intrude". This approach has not been universally accepted, and has been described as old-fashioned since the 1940s, while film historian Donald McCaffrey sees it as an indication that Chaplin never fully understood the medium of film. Nevertheless, Kamin argues that Chaplin's comic talent would never have been enough to keep him funny on screen if he hadn't had "the ability to conceive and direct scenes specifically for the cinema".

Music

From childhood, Chaplin developed a passion for music, and taught himself to play the piano, violin and cello. He considered the musical accompaniment an integral part of the film, and from *L'Opinion publique* onwards he devoted a great deal of time to this field. He composed the soundtrack for *Lumières de la ville* himself, and did the same for all his subsequent films; from the late 1950s until his death, he provided soundtracks for all his earlier silent shorts.

As he had no musical education, Chaplin never knew how to read or write scores. He therefore called on professional composers such as David Raksin, Raymond Rasch and Eric James to shape his ideas. Some critics have argued that the music for his films should be attributed to the composers who worked with him; Raksin, who helped set the music for Les *Temps Modernes*, nevertheless emphasized Chaplin's creative and driving role in the composition process. At the start of this work, which can last months, Chaplin describes exactly what he wants to the composers and plays the elements he has improvised on the piano. These melodies are then developed in close collaboration. For film historian Jeffrey Vance, "even if he relied on his associates to shape complex instrumentations, the musical instructions were his own, and not a note was placed without his approval".

Chaplin's compositions gave rise to three popular songs. *Smile*, composed for *Les Temps modernes, was later set to* lyrics by John Turner and Geoffrey Parsons, and performed by Nat King Cole in 1954. For *Les Feux de la rampe*, Chaplin composed *Terry's Theme*, which was popularized by Jimmy Young under the title *Eternally* in 1952. Finally, the song *This Is My Song*, sung by Petula Clark for *The Countess of Hong Kong*, was a great commercial success, reaching number one in the British charts in 1967. Apart from his two honorary awards, the only Oscar Chaplin won was for Best Film Score on the occasion of the 1973 re-release of Les *Feux de la rampe* .

Filmography

With the publication of his autobiography, Chaplin set out his filmography, which now consists of 80 films (*The Countess of Hong Kong,* made three years later, was later added). In 2010, a copy of *La Course au voleur (The Thief's Run)*, made in 1914 and previously considered lost, was discovered in an antique shop in Michigan, bringing his filmography to 82 films.

Chaplin's films, up to and including Le *Cirque*, are silent, although some have been reissued with soundtracks. *City Lights* and *Modern Times* are silent, but include soundtracks composed of music, sound effects and spoken sequences for the latter. Chaplin's last five films were talkies. With the exception of *The Countess of Hong Kong*, all Chaplin's films are shot in 35 mm, black-and-white format.

In French, Jacques Dumesnil doubled Chaplin in *Monsieur Verdoux*, *Les Feux de la rampe* and *Un roi à New York*. Chaplin was also dubbed by Henri Virlogeux in the 1942 sound version of *La Ruée vers l'or*, in 1968 by Roger Carel in *Le Dictateur* and by Jean-Henri Chambois in *La Comtesse de Hong-Kong*.

Feature films :

- 1921: *The Kid*
- 1923: *L'Opinion publique*
- 1925: *The Gold Rush*
- 1928: *The Circus*
- 1931: *City Lights*
- 1936: *Modern Times*
- 1940: *The Dictator*
- 1947: *Monsieur Verdoux*
- 1952 : *Les Feux de la rampe*
- 1957: *A King in New York*
- 1967: *The Countess of Hong Kong*

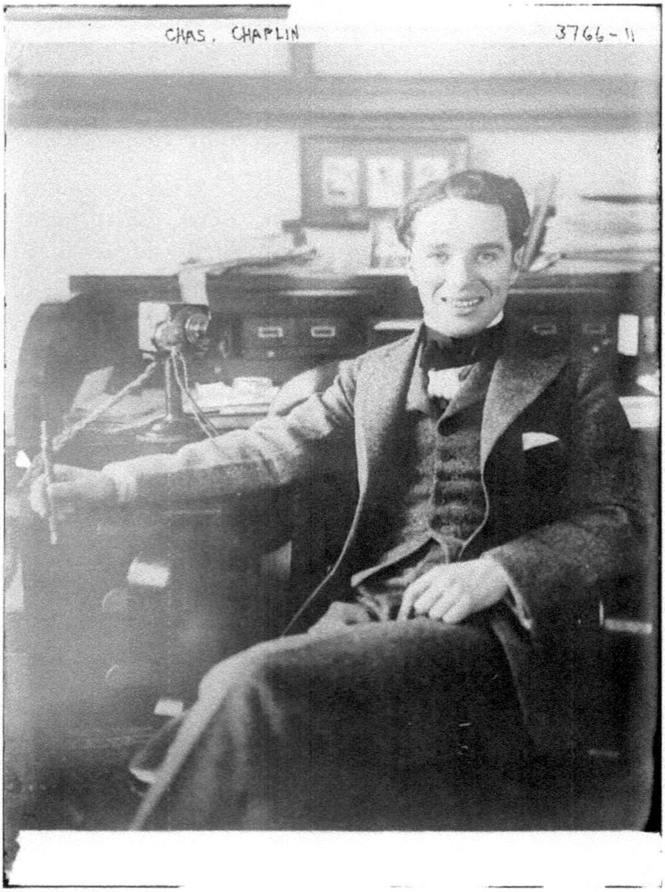
CHAS. CHAPLIN
3766-11

Recognition

Awards

Chaplin received numerous awards and distinctions, particularly at the end of his life. In 1962, the universities of Durham and Oxford awarded him the honorary degree of Doctor of Letters. In 1965, he shared the Erasmus Prize with Ingmar Bergman, and in 1971 was made Commander of the National Order of the Legion of Honor by the French government. In 1975, he was knighted by Queen Elizabeth II and made a Commander of the Order of the British Empire, becoming "Sir Charles Chaplin".

The film industry rewarded him with a special Golden Lion at the 1972 Venice Film Festival, as well as a star on the Hollywood Walk of Fame in 1970 (he had previously been refused because of his political views).

Chaplin received a total of three Oscars: his first Honorary Oscar in 1929 "for his versatility and genius in acting, writing, directing and producing *Le Cirque*"; a second in 1972 "for the incalculable effect he has had in making motion pictures the art form of this century"; and a third in 1973 for Best Original Score (jointly with Ray Rasch and Larry Russell), for *Les Feux de la Rampe*. He was also nominated in the Best Actor, Best Film and Best

Screenplay categories for *Le Dictateur, as well as* Best Screenplay for *Monsieur Verdoux*.

Six of Chaplin's films have been selected for preservation in the National Film Registry of the U.S. Library of Congress: *The Emigrant* (1917), *The Kid* (1921), *The Gold Rush* (1925), *City Lights* (1931), *Modern Times* (1936) and *The Great Dictator* (1940).

Posterity

In 1998, critic Andrew Sarris wrote that Chaplin is "arguably the greatest artist cinema has created, certainly its most extraordinary performer and probably still its most universal icon". He is described by the British Film Institute as "a tutelary figure of world culture", and *Time* magazine listed him among the 100 most important people of the XXe century for "the laughter [he brought] to millions" and because he "more or less invented worldwide fame and helped transform an industry into an art form".

Film historian Christian Hansmeyer notes that the image of Charlie Chaplin is part of cultural history; according to Simon Louvish, the character is known even in places where his films have never been shown. Critic Richard Schickel suggests that Chaplin's films with Charlie Chaplin present "the most eloquent and richest comic expressions of the human spirit" in the history of cinema. Objects associated with the character continue to fascinate audiences, and in 2006, a bowler hat and bamboo walking stick that once belonged to Chaplin were bought for $140,000 at an auction in Los Angeles.

As a director, Chaplin is considered a pioneer and one of the most influential figures of the early 20th[e] century[''']. Film historian Mark Cousins has written that Chaplin "changed not only the imagery of cinema, but also its sociology and grammar", and argues that he played an important role in establishing comedy as a genre, alongside what D. W. Griffith had done for drama. He was the first to popularize feature-length comedy, and to slow down the pace of the action to add finesse and pathos'. For Robinson, Chaplin's innovations were "rapidly assimilated and became the basic practices of filmmaking". Federico Fellini (who defines Chaplin as "a kind of Adam from whom we all came"), Jacques Tati ("without him, I'd never have made a film"), René Clair ("he inspired practically every director"), Michael Powell, Billy Wilder and Richard Attenborough are among the directors who claim to have been influenced by Chaplin.

Chaplin also inspired avant-garde poets of the XXe century, as well as future comedians such as Marcel Marceau, who said he decided to become a mime after seeing him, and Raj Kapoor, who based his acting on that of Charlie Chaplin. Mark Cousins has also identified

Chaplin's comic style in the French Monsieur Hulot and Italian Totò, not to mention his influence on cartoon characters such as Felix the Cat and Mickey Mouse. As a founding member of United Artists, Chaplin played an important role in the development of the film industry. Gerald Mast noted that while this company never rivaled MGM or Paramount, the idea of directors producing their own films was "far ahead of its time".

On the occasion of the 1958 Brussels World's Fair, an international jury of 117 critics established a ranking of the best films of all time: *The Gold Rush* (1925) came second behind Sergei Eisenstein's *Battleship Potemkin* (1925) and ahead of Vittorio De Sica's *Bicycle Thief* (1948). Many of Chaplin's films are still considered among the greatest ever made. British magazine *Sight and Sound*'s 2012 list of the best films in history, conducted among film critics, lists *City Lights*, *Modern Times*, *The Great Dictator* and *The Gold Rush* at 50^e , 63^e , 144^e and 154^e respectively; the same survey of directors puts *Modern Times at* 22^e , *City Lights* at 30^e and *The Gold Rush* at 91^e . In 2007, the American Film Institute named *City Lights* the 11^e greatest American film of all time, while *The Gold Rush* and *Modern Times were* in the top 100.

Tributes

In April 2016, Ban's mansion in Corsier-sur-Vevey, Switzerland, where he spent the last twenty-five years of his life, became a museum dedicated to his life and work. The museum, called "*Chaplin's World*", is the fruit of a partnership between Compagnie des Alpes (CDA), Genii Capital and Chaplin Museum Development (CMD). The commune of Corsier-sur-Vevey has named a park after him, and a stele commemorates the illustrious resident.

The neighboring town of Vevey named a square in his honor on Quai Perdonnet, on the shores of Lake Geneva, and in 1982 erected a statue of Chaplin, the work of British sculptor John Doubleday. To the north of the town, a few hundred metres from the Manoir de Ban, two 14-storey buildings have been decorated with frescoes evoking the artist's career.

The Irish town of Waterville, where Chaplin spent several summers with his family in the 1960s, has hosted the annual Charlie Chaplin Comedy Film Festival since 2011, designed to honor the comedian's legacy and discover new talent. Among other tributes, a minor planet, (3623) Chaplin, was named in his honor in 1981 by Soviet astronomer Lyudmila Karatchkina, and numerous countries have issued stamps bearing his effigy.

Chaplin's legacy is managed by the Chaplin Association, founded by several of his children, which owns the copyright to his image, name and most films made after 1918. The Cinematheque in Bologna, Italy, houses the Association's main archives, including images, manuscripts and letters. Over 10,000 photographs of his life and career are also stored at the Musée de l'Élysée in Lausanne, Switzerland. In the UK, the Cinema Museum in south London is considered "the nearest thing to a Chaplin museum Britain has" by Charlie Chaplin's family. The British Film Institute founded the Charles Chaplin Research Foundation, which organized the first international conference on the filmmaker in London in July 2005.

Chaplin was the subject of a biographical film directed by Richard Attenborough, *Chaplin*, in 1992; he is played by Robert Downey Jr. who was nominated for an Oscar for Best Actor and won the BAFTA for Best Actor. He was also played by Eddie Izzard in the film *A Scent of Murder* (2001). A TV series about Chaplin's childhood, *Young Charlie Chaplin, was* broadcast by PBS in 1989 and nominated for an Emmy Award for Best Children's Program.

Xavier Beauvois' 2014 film *La Rançon de la gloire,* starring Benoît Poelvoorde and Roschdy Zem, is loosely based on the theft of Charlie Chaplin's remains in 1978. Bernard Swysen recounts his life in a comic strip entitled *Charlie Chaplin, les étoiles de l'histoire*, drawn by Bruno Bazile and published in October 2019. In 2021, François Aymé and Yves Jeuland will produce the documentary *Charlie Chaplin, le génie de la liberté*.

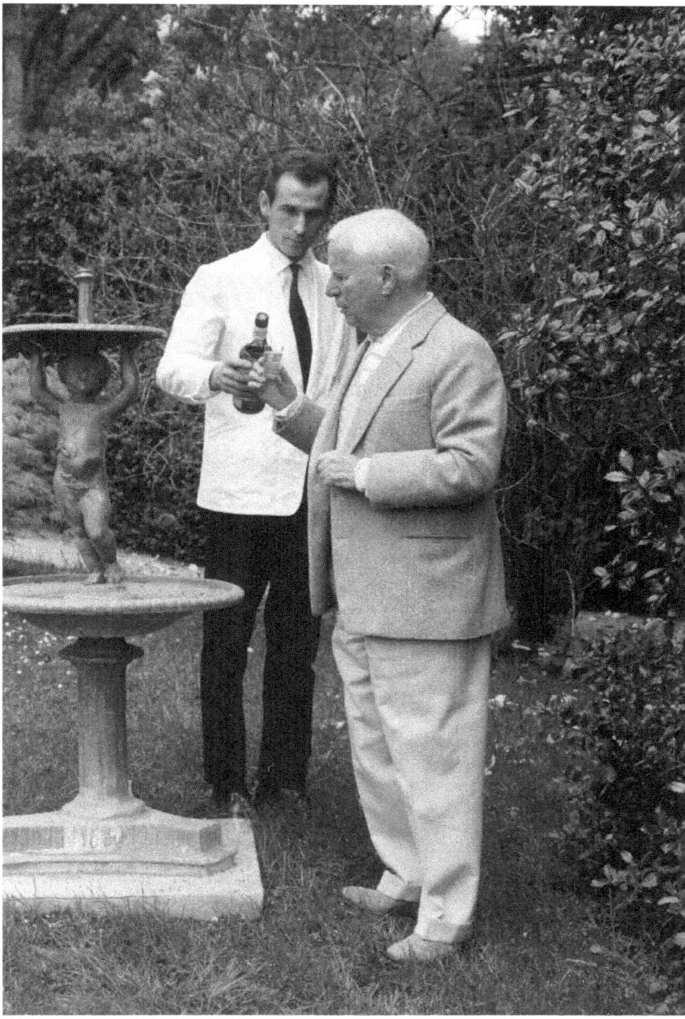

Other books by United Library

https://campsite.bio/unitedlibrary

Milton Keynes UK
Ingram Content Group UK Ltd.
UKHW021117031224
452078UK00011B/919